love
poems f
m

Printed in the United States of America

First Printing, 2021

ISBN: 978-1-7347545-9-9

Press Here
410 S Michigan Ave Suite 420
Chicago, IL 60605

www.mattbodett.com

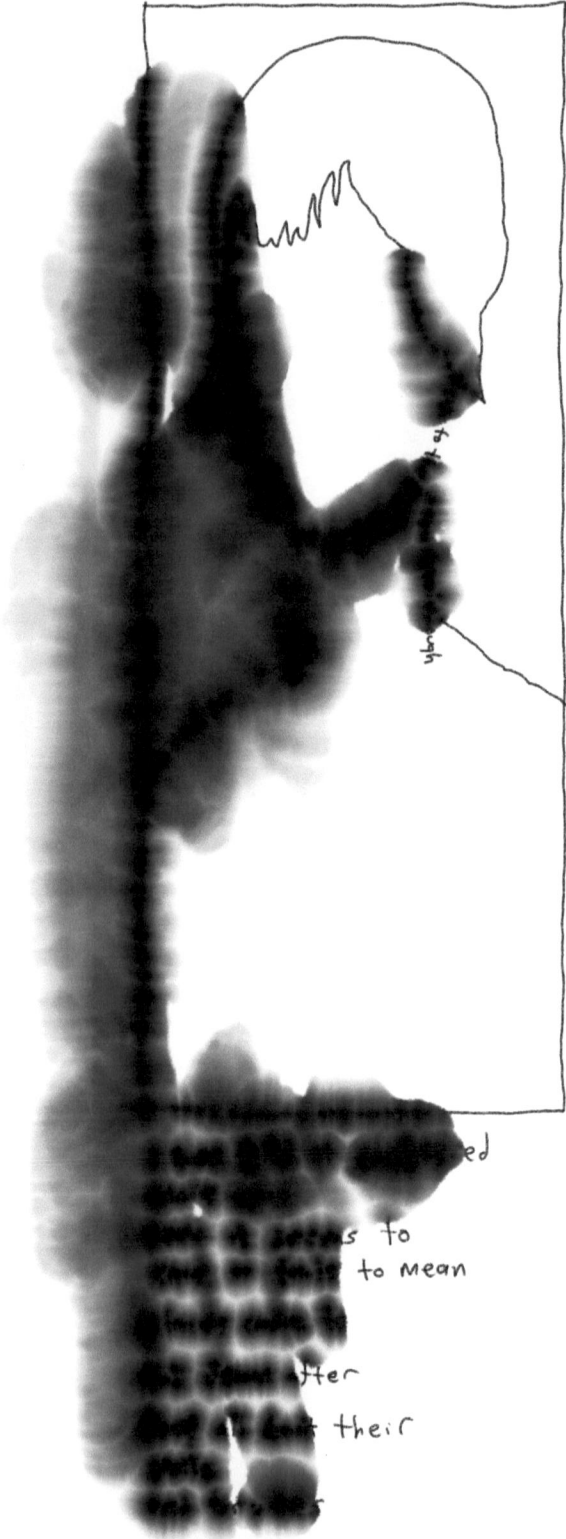

ed

s to
to mean

fter

their

songs are not this empty

places like this don't
remember

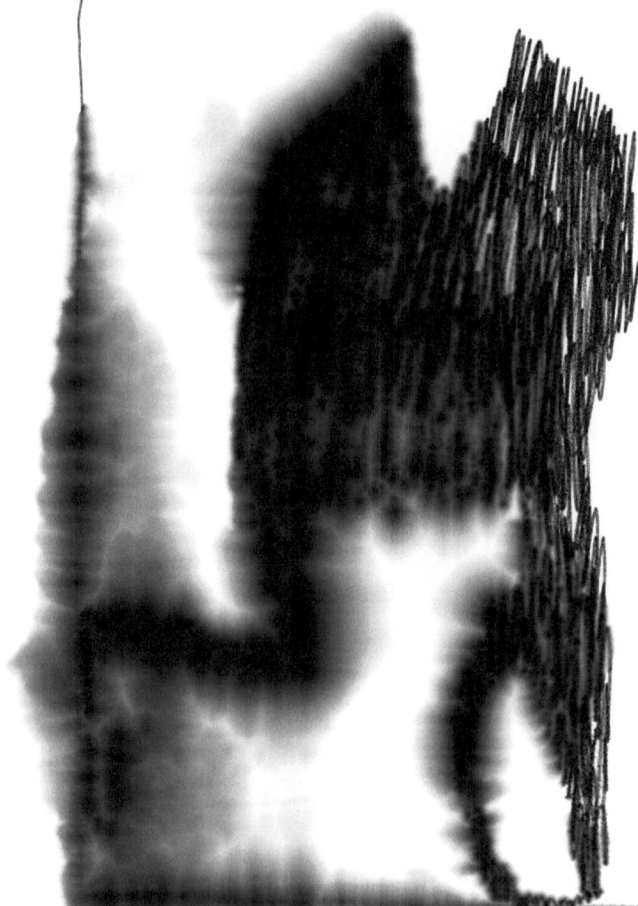

just like
more to far needs

carry sad

it is   about
                         that

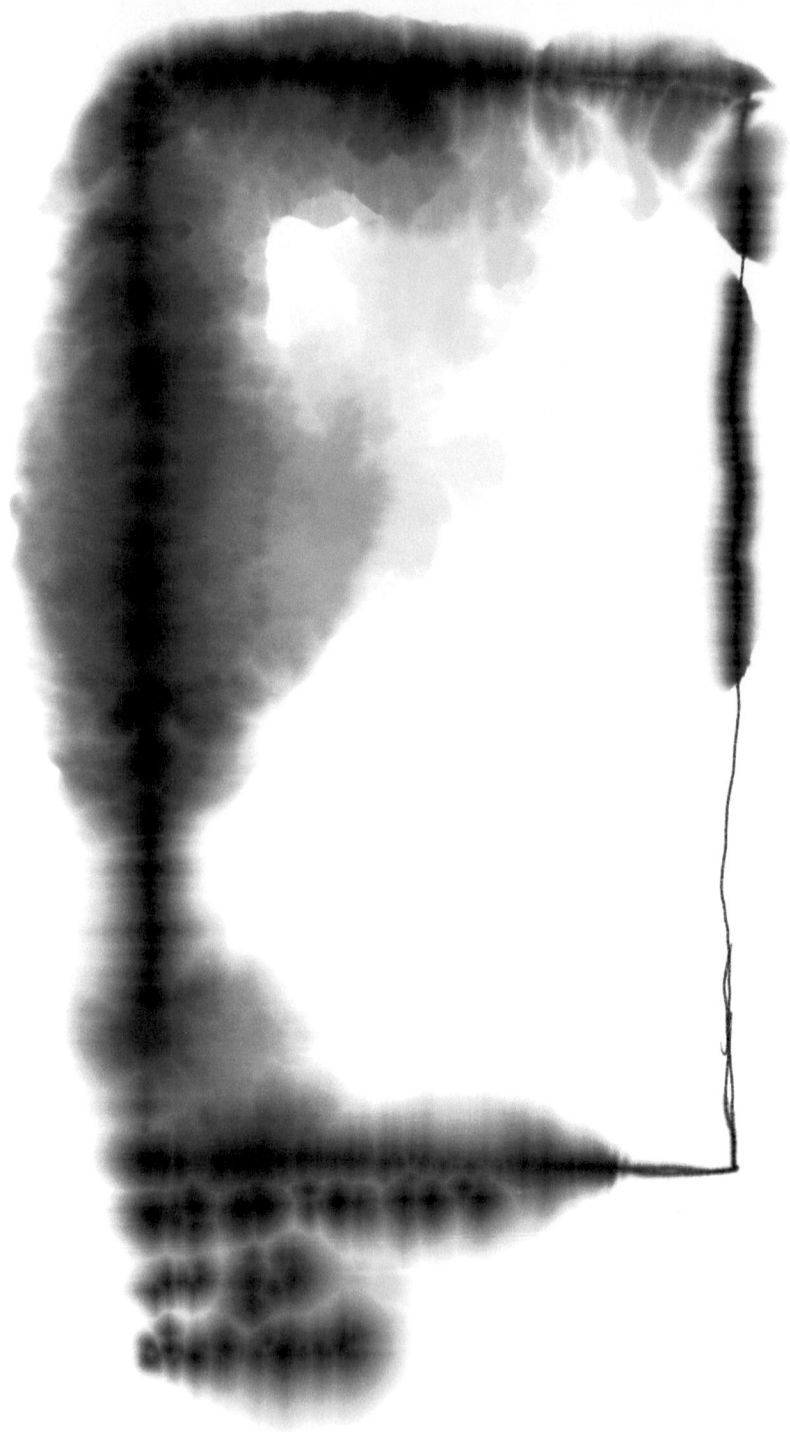

as   if   one

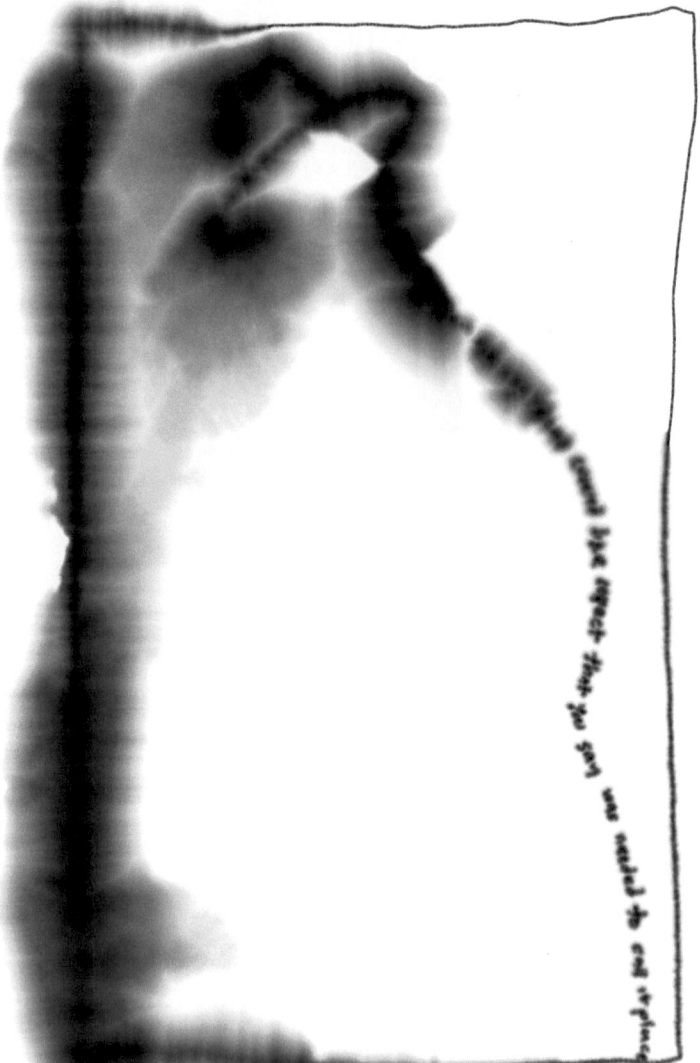

broke   home
          sick

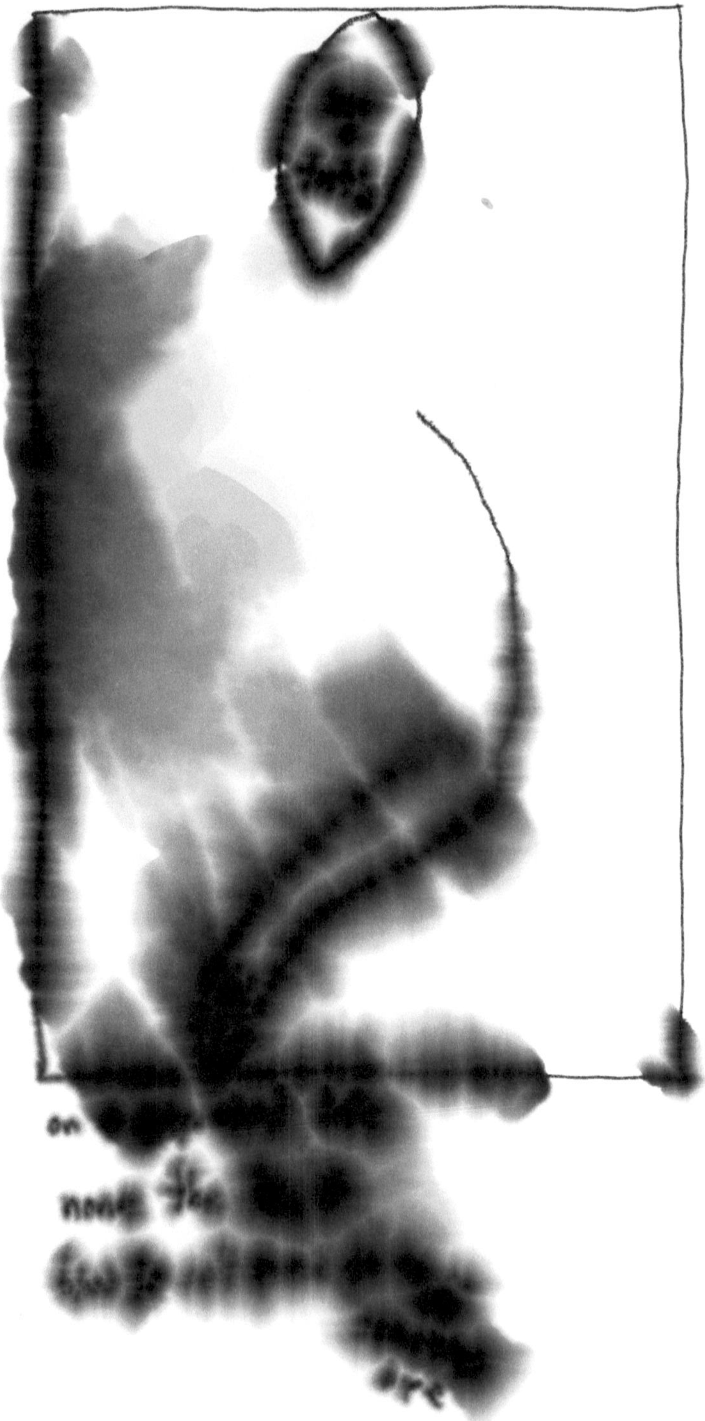
on
none the
are

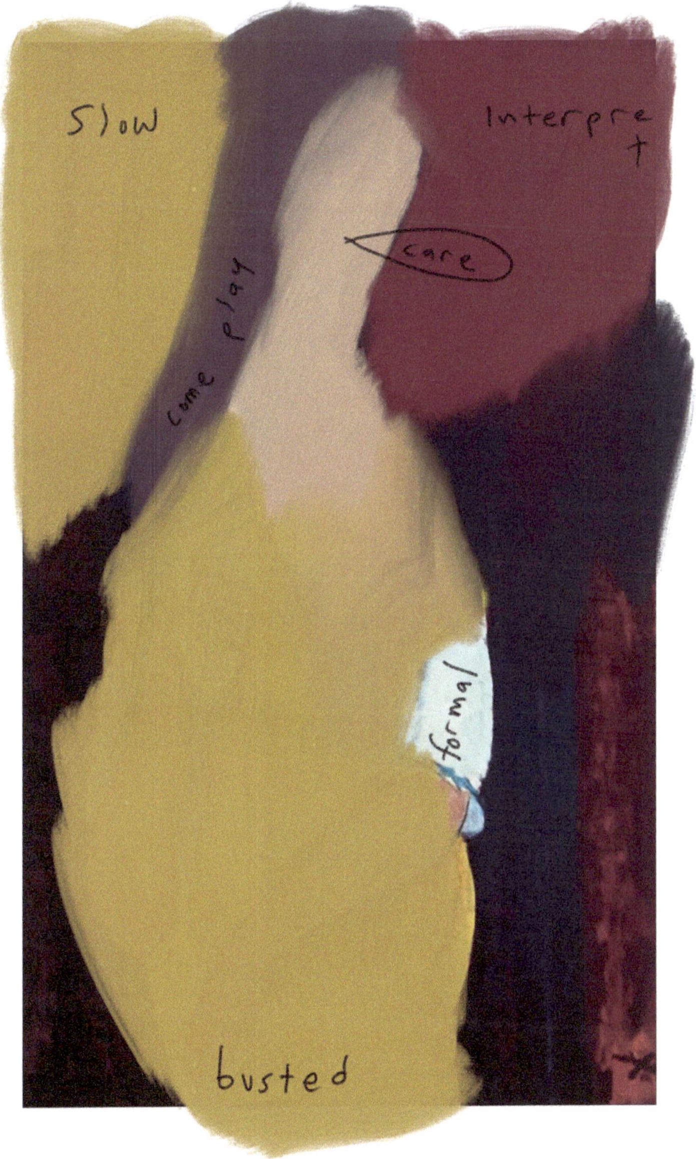
slow
interpret
care
come play
formal
busted

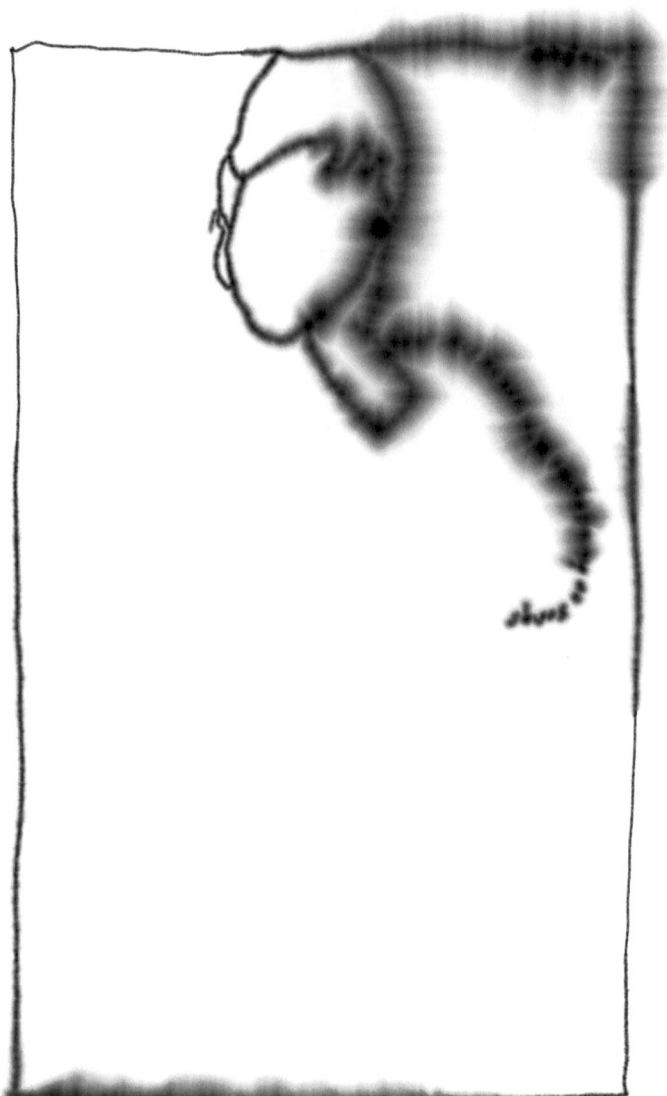

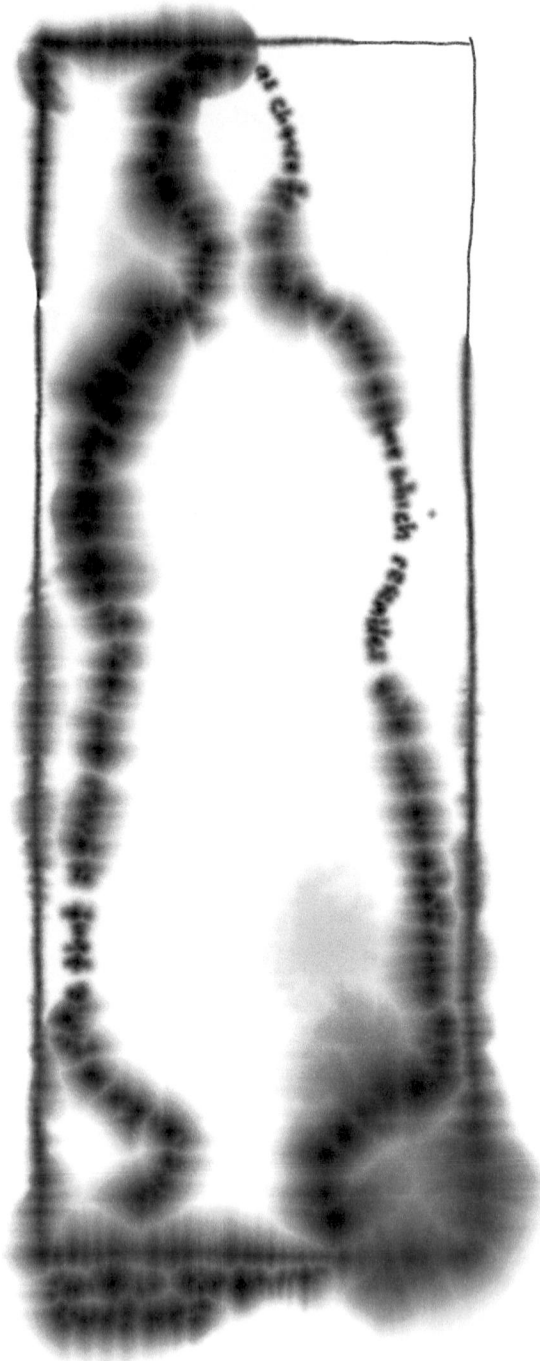

ROCOCO

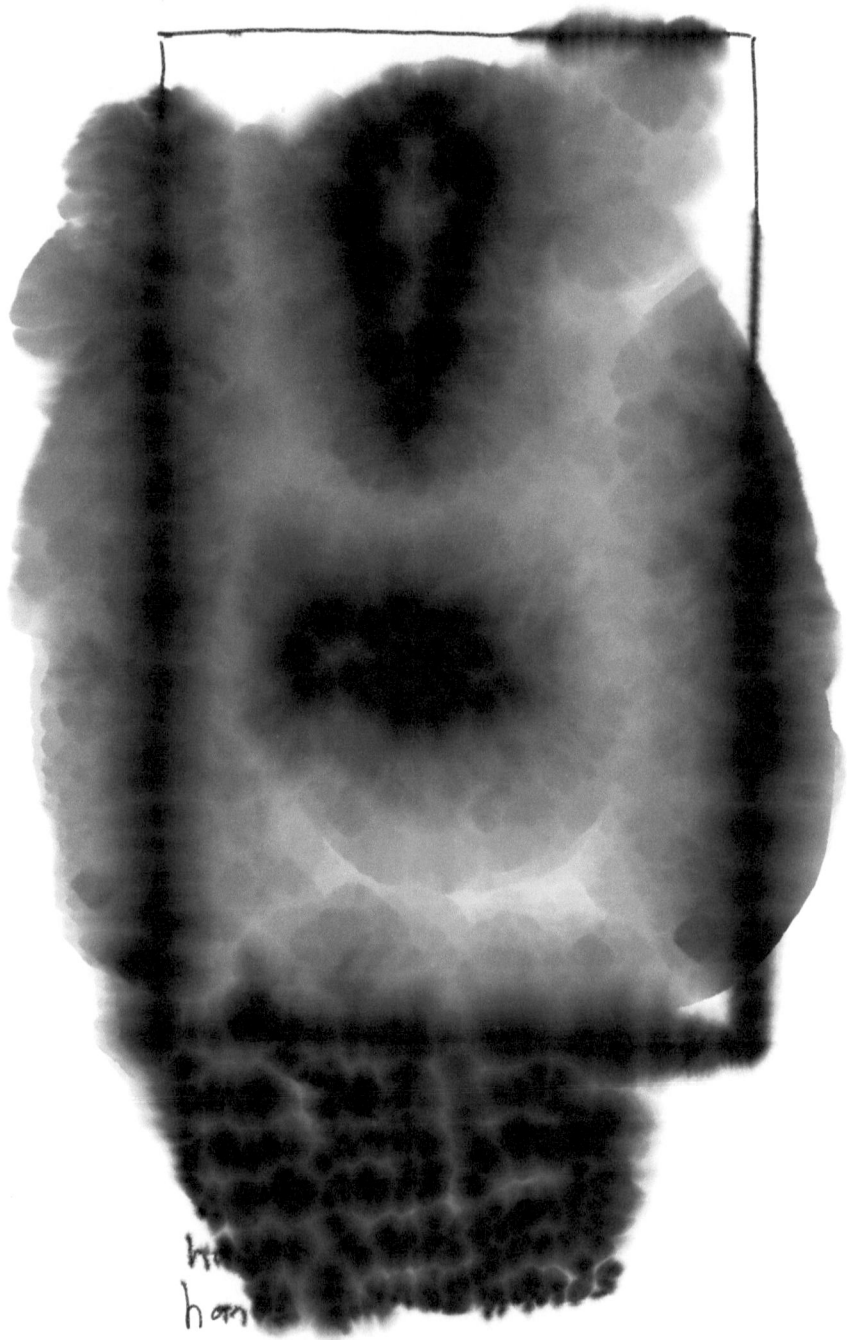

han

mine

whole

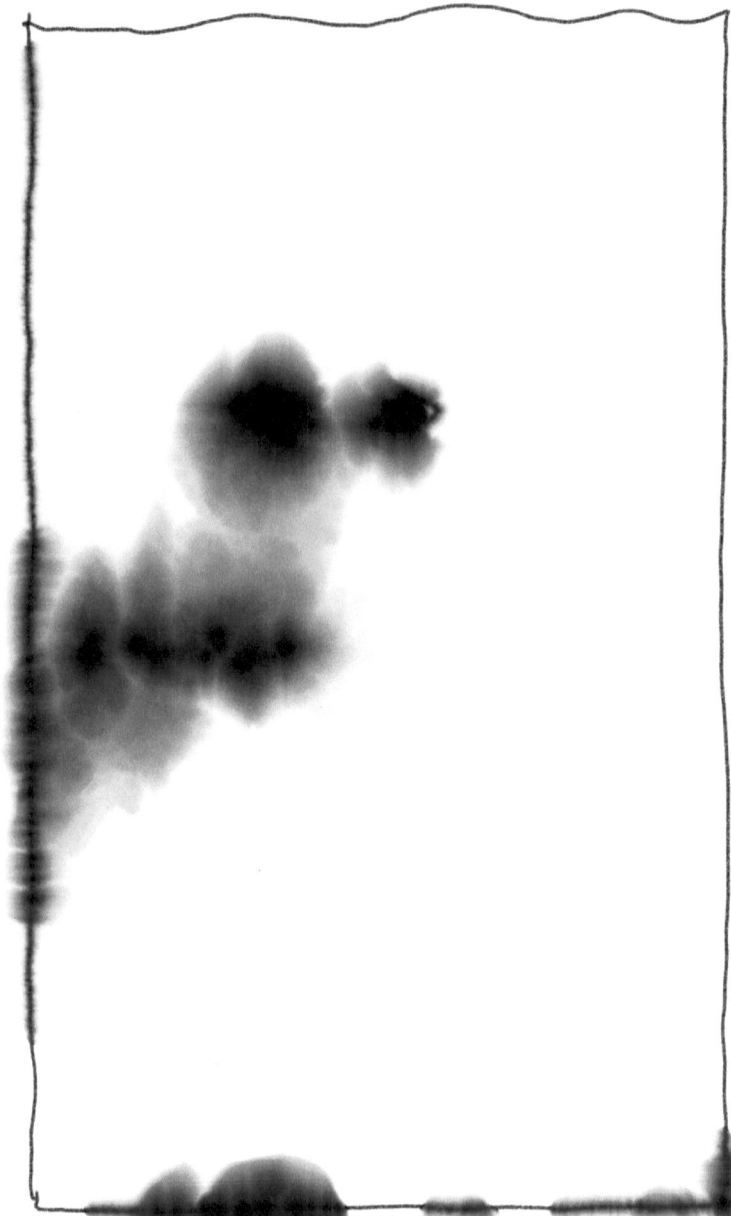

note
u
re   foghy
li

small

torn
torn

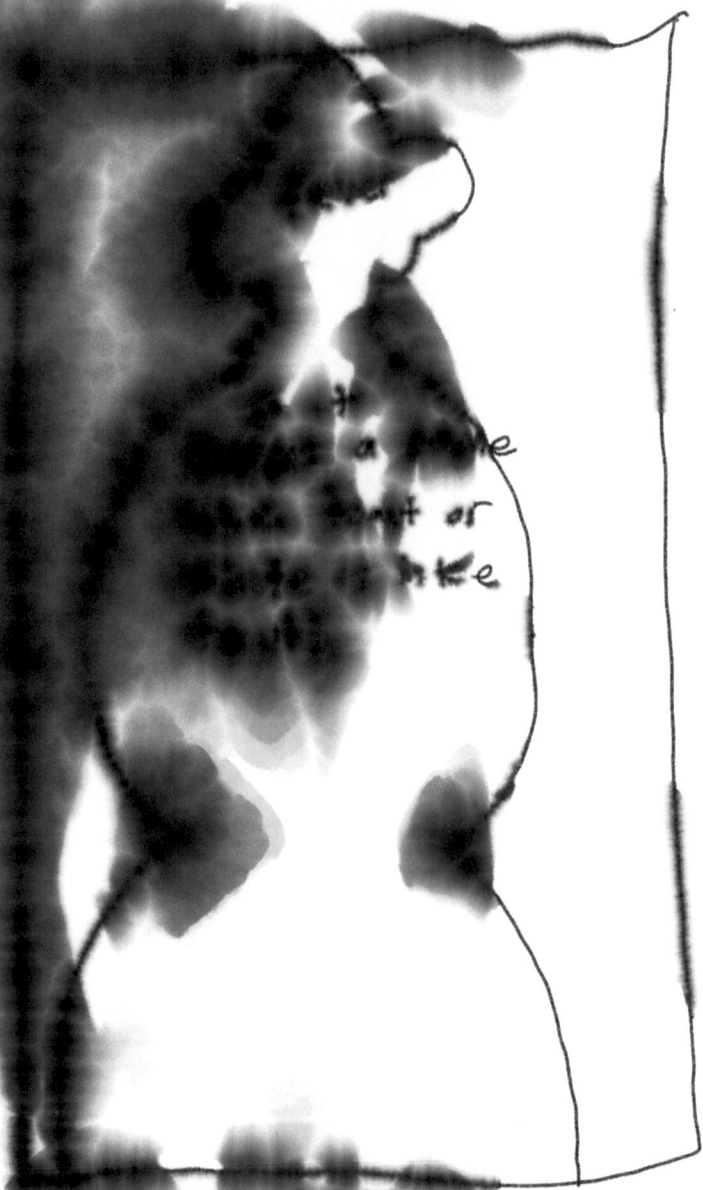

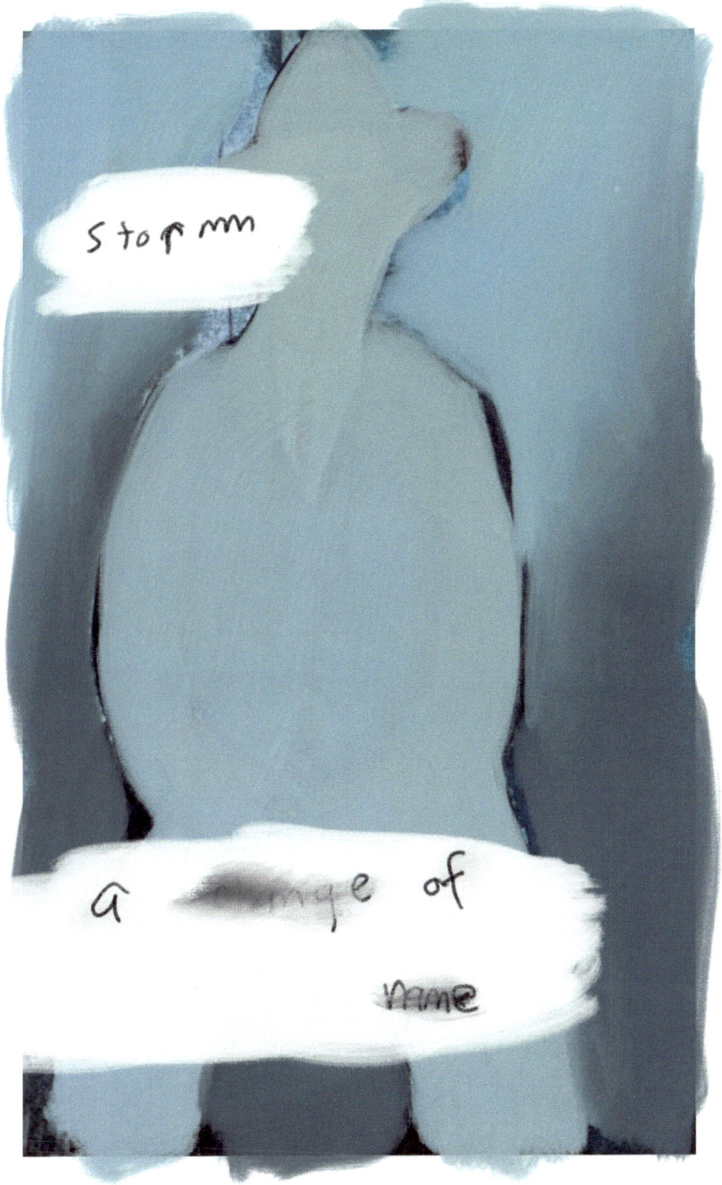

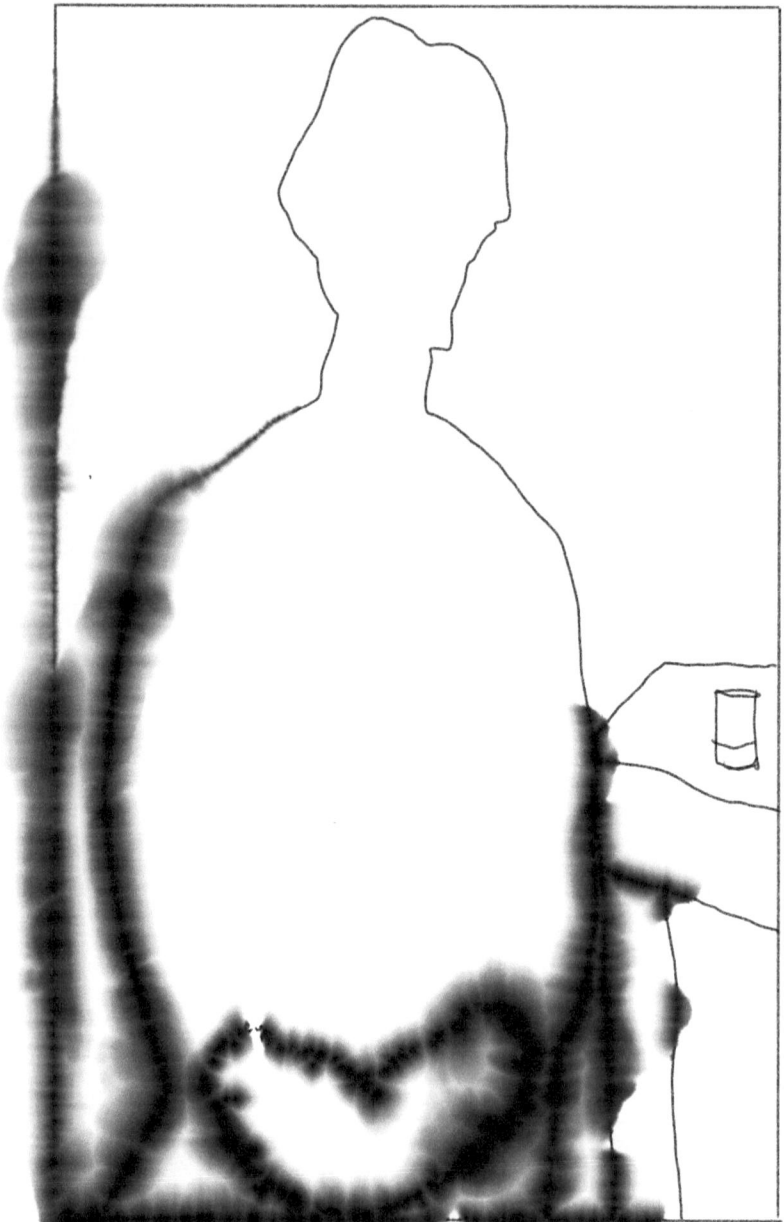

Small Breasts

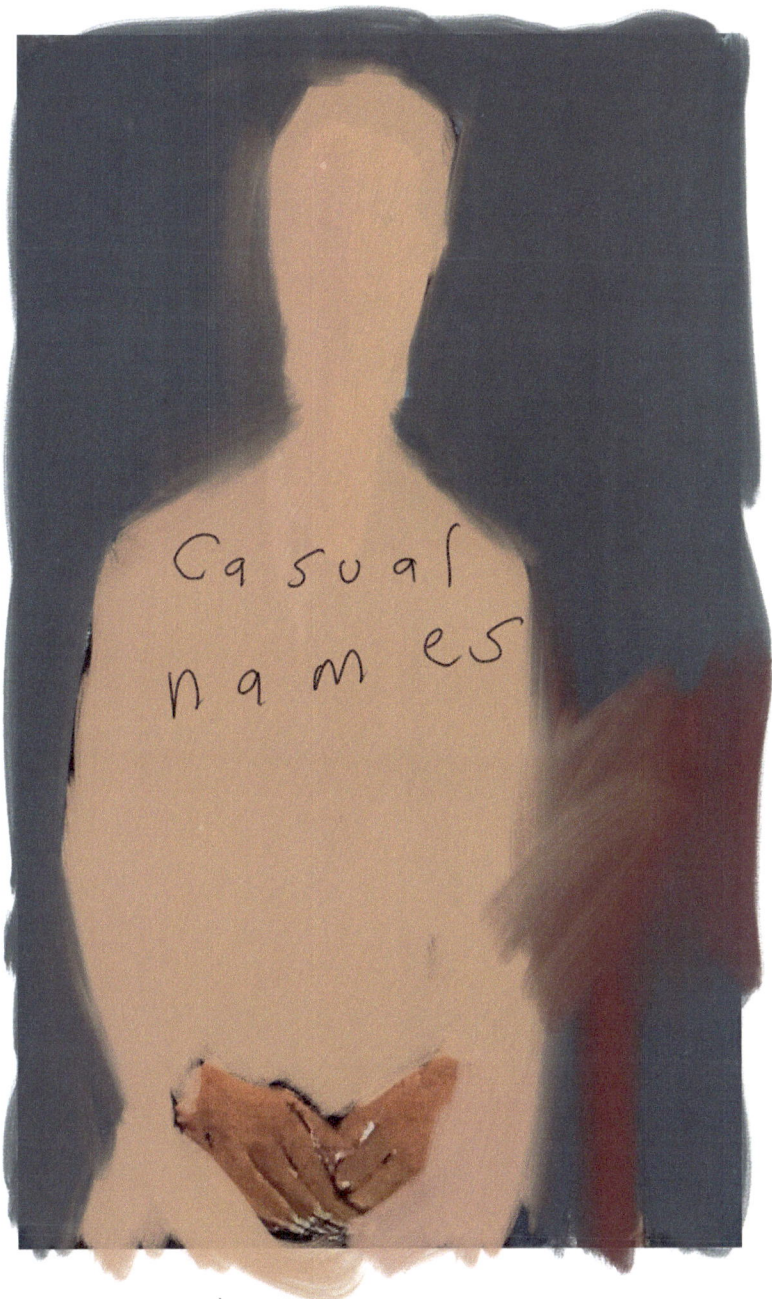

Casual
names

in a pill form

each year
like slipping
with catapaults
catastrophe

familiar

Sounds   Sounds
                          sounds

sometimes it is the same bruise

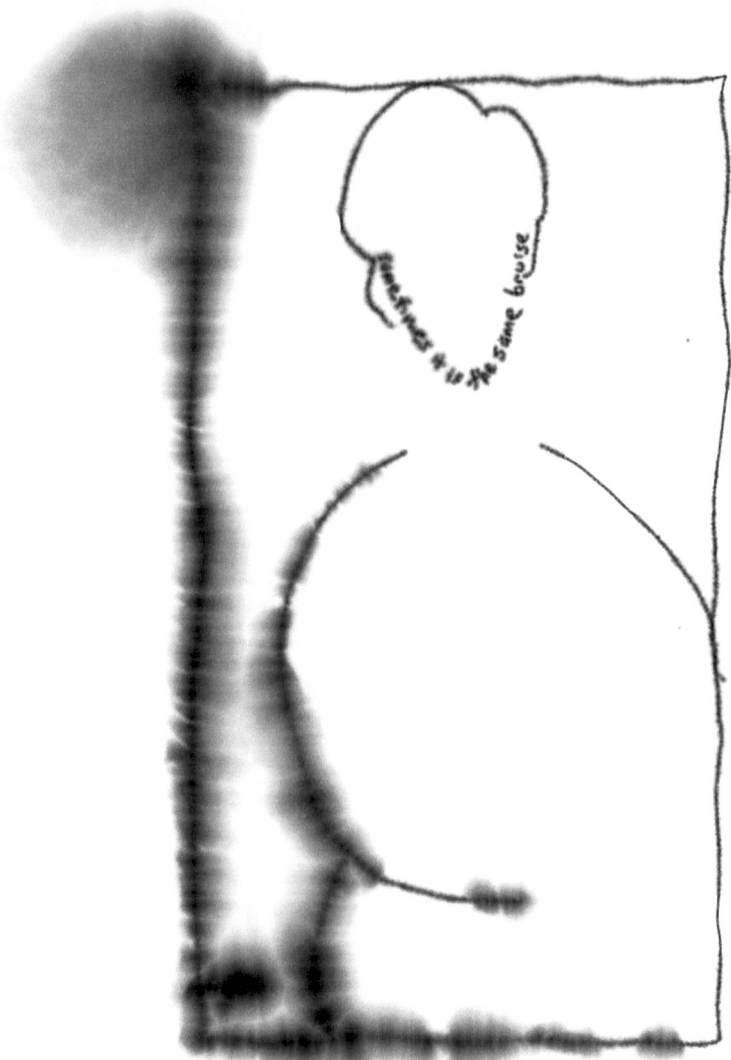

perhaps more memory
than
parade.

it isn't

for
getting

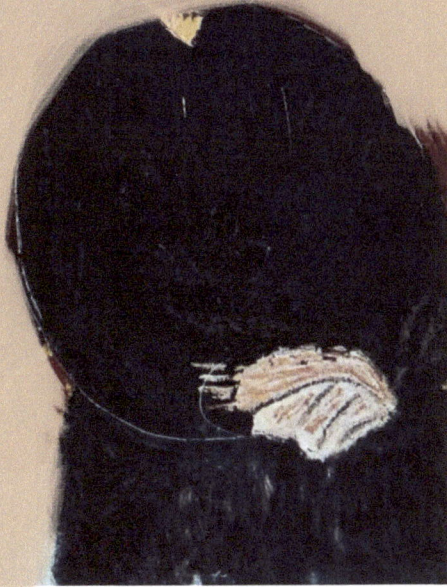

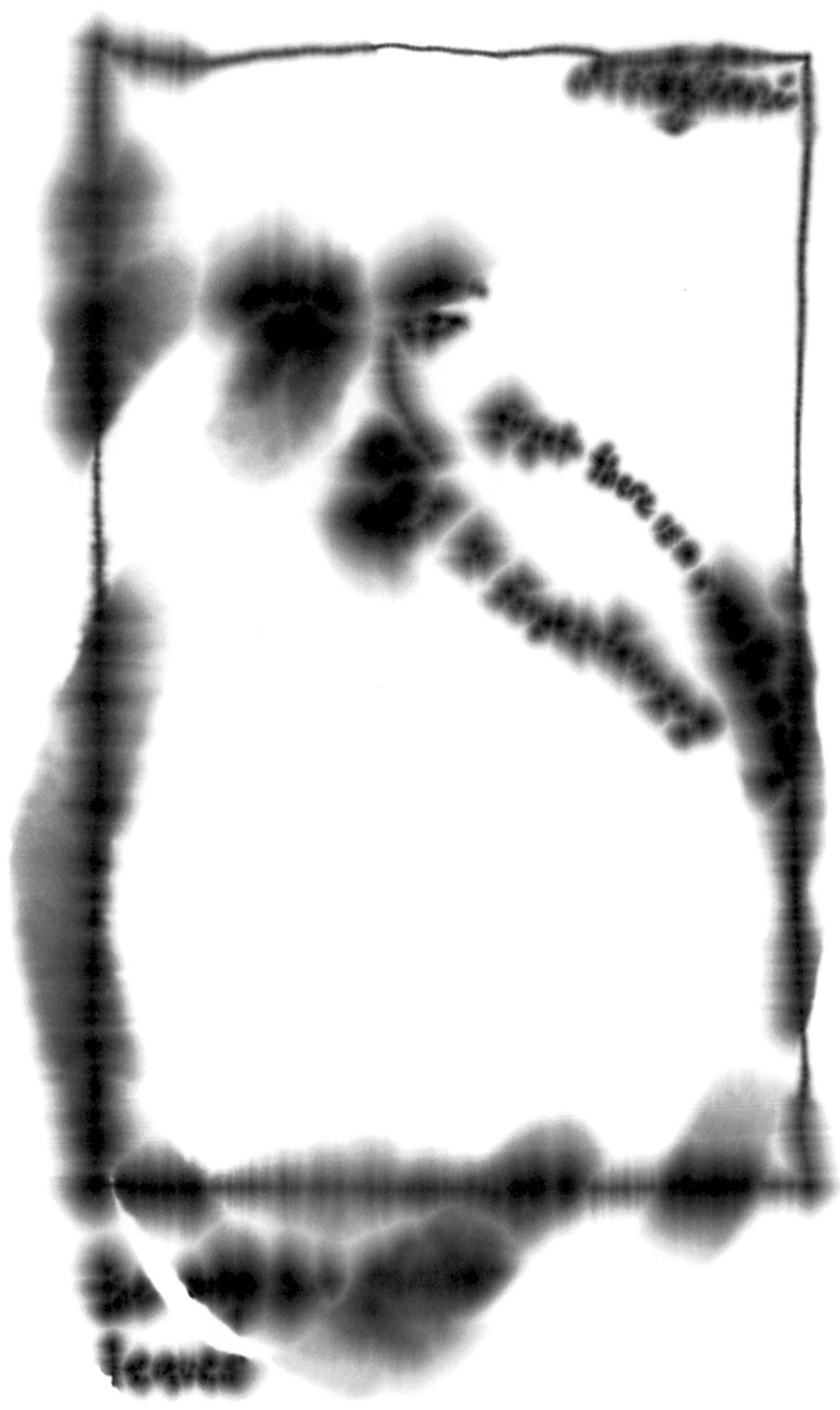

this
ends

resistance
and

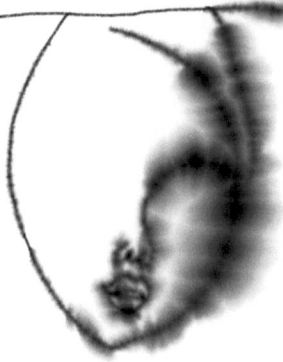

MCLENNI

each five
to occupy

s o
for
mal

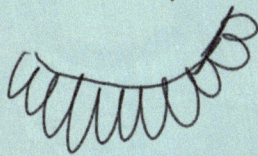

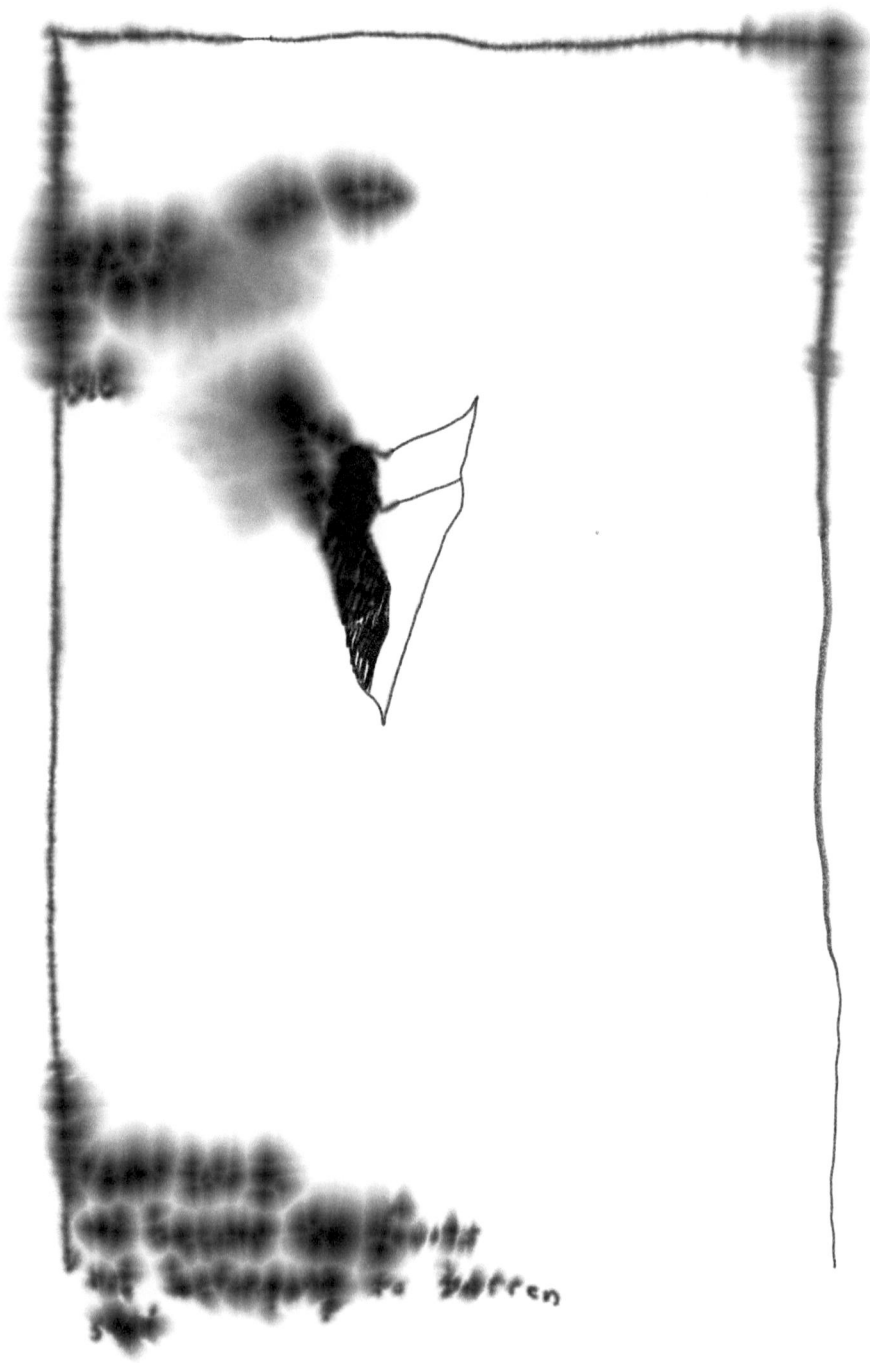

dress to impress

role   role

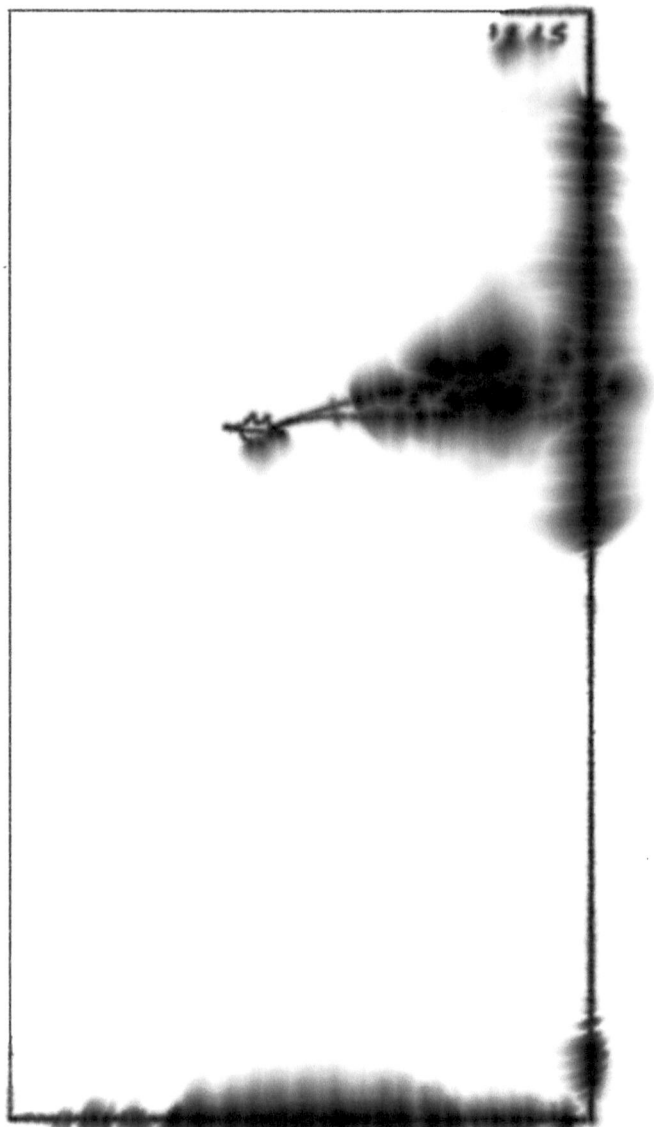

IS

can

or

feels

similar

reasons   have

reasons

been telling

did you   mean

seeing   dust

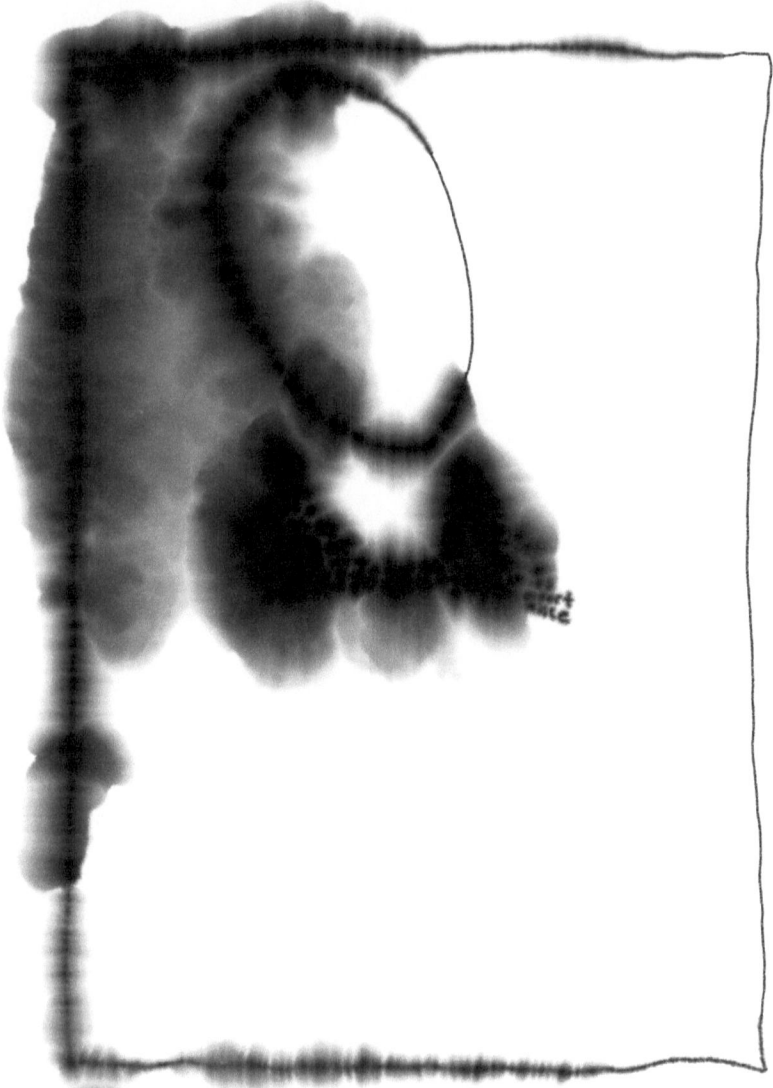

something about alone

Individual ™

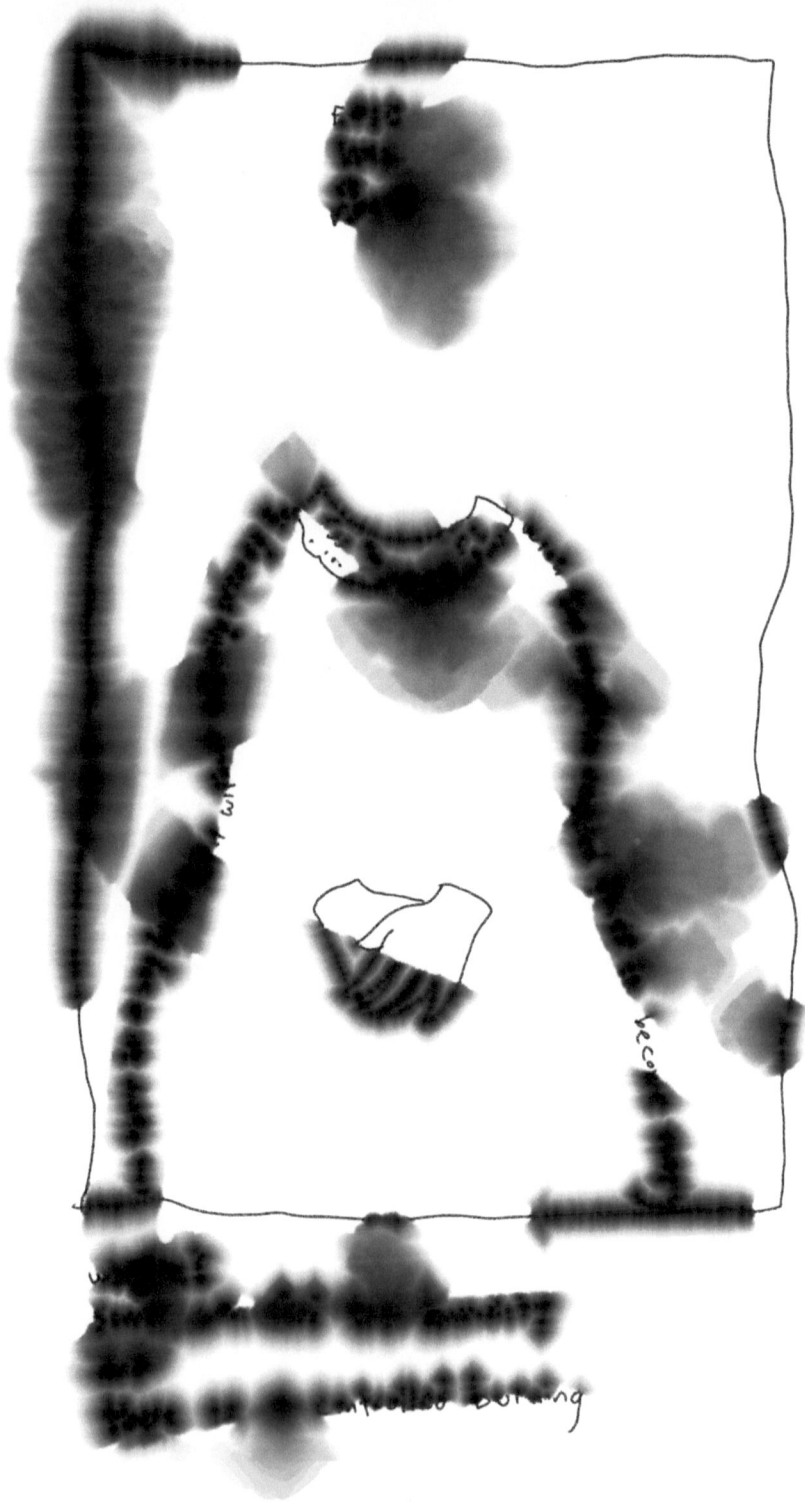

epic

and   formal

past

why
like   is a
                                    thinking

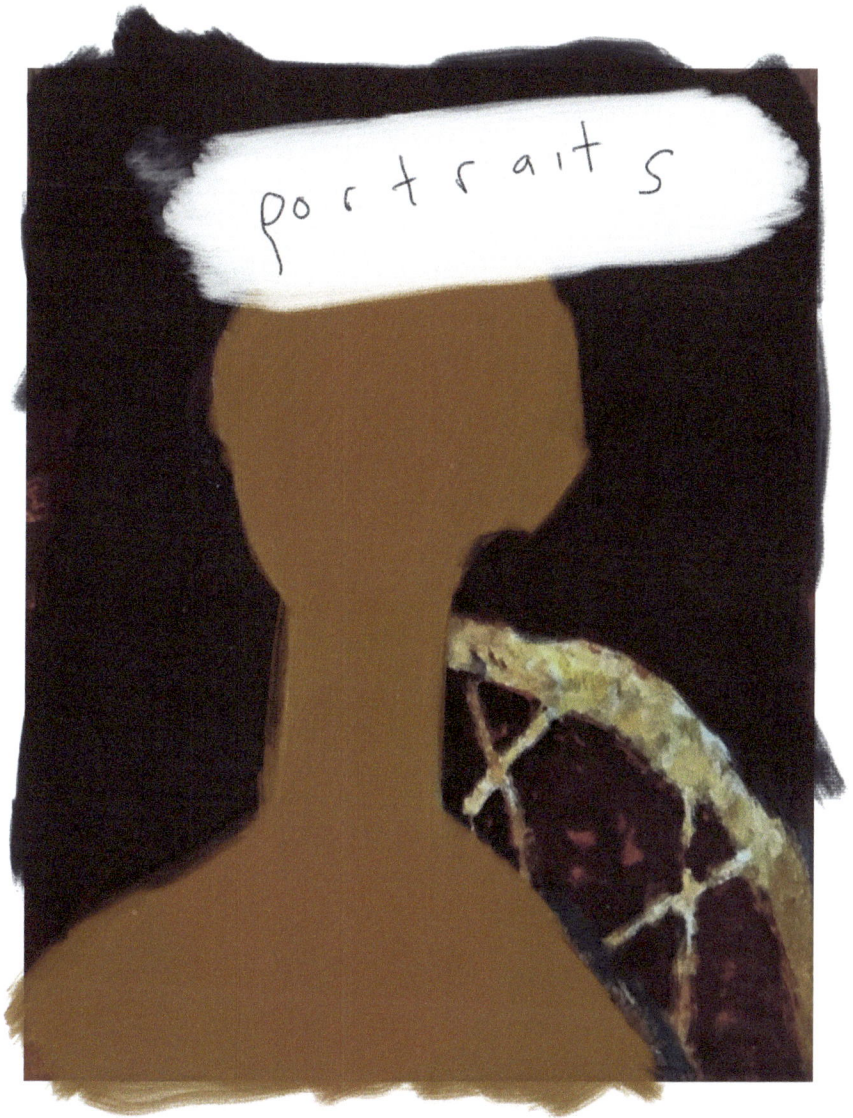

portraits

(sometimes©) price

looking

location
location
locatron

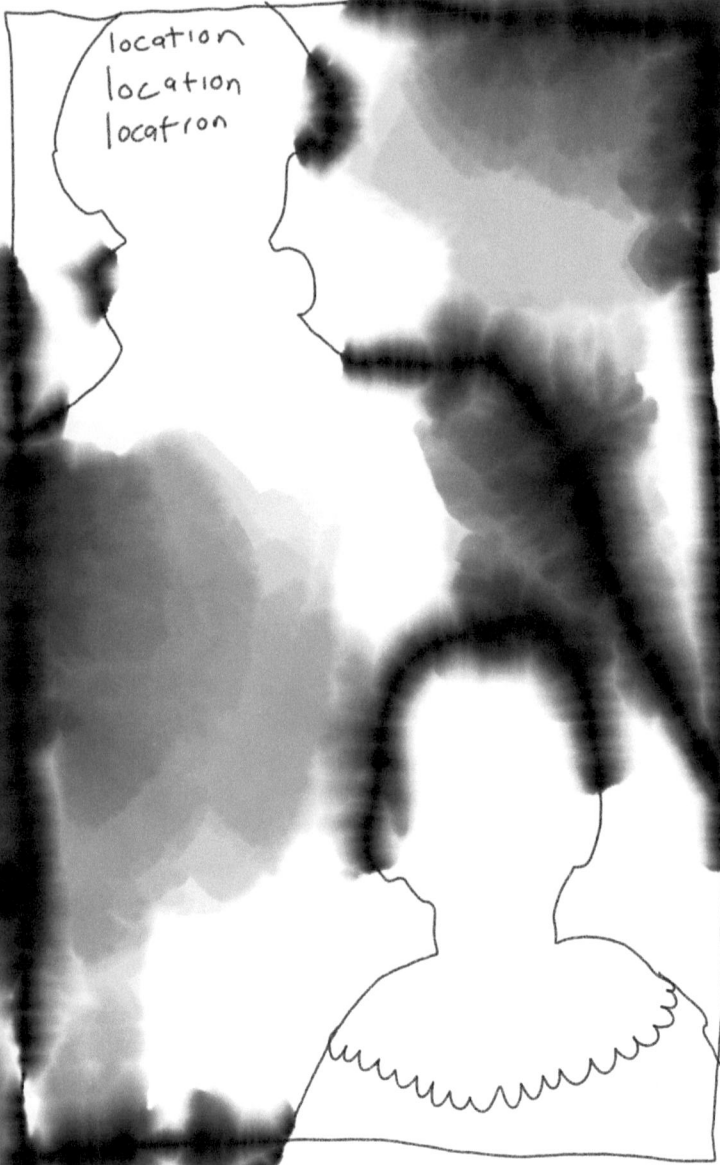

to
titles
and dications
ace

Sea

lost each of the cast
to melancholy

Some ... t te... ...ories that offer collisions

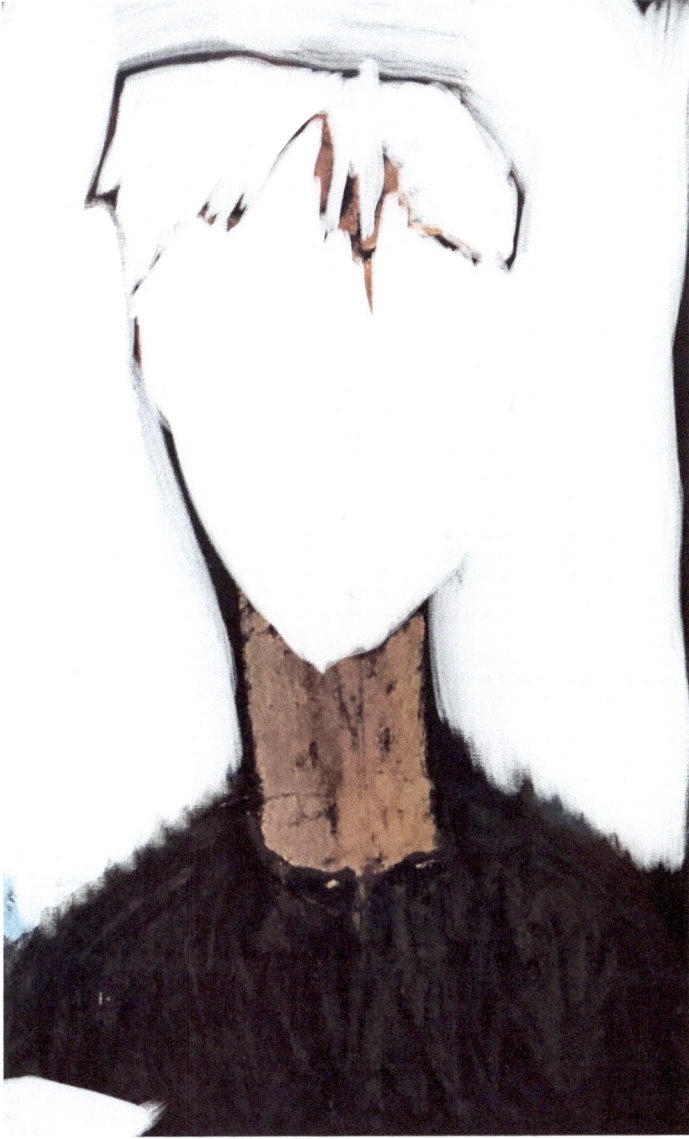

the same as importance

adam

I to holding
the
hold
way to remain

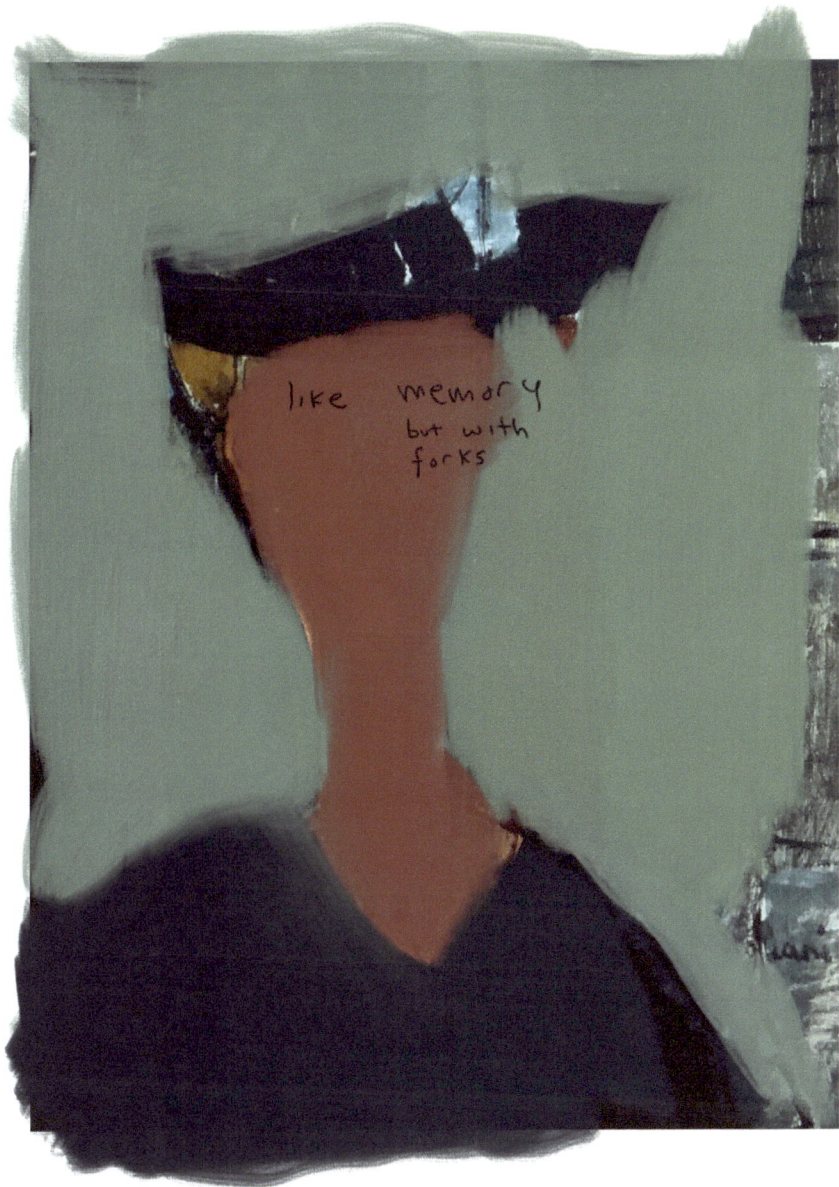

like memory
but with
forks

single   single